REGIONS OF AMERICA

NEW ENGLAND

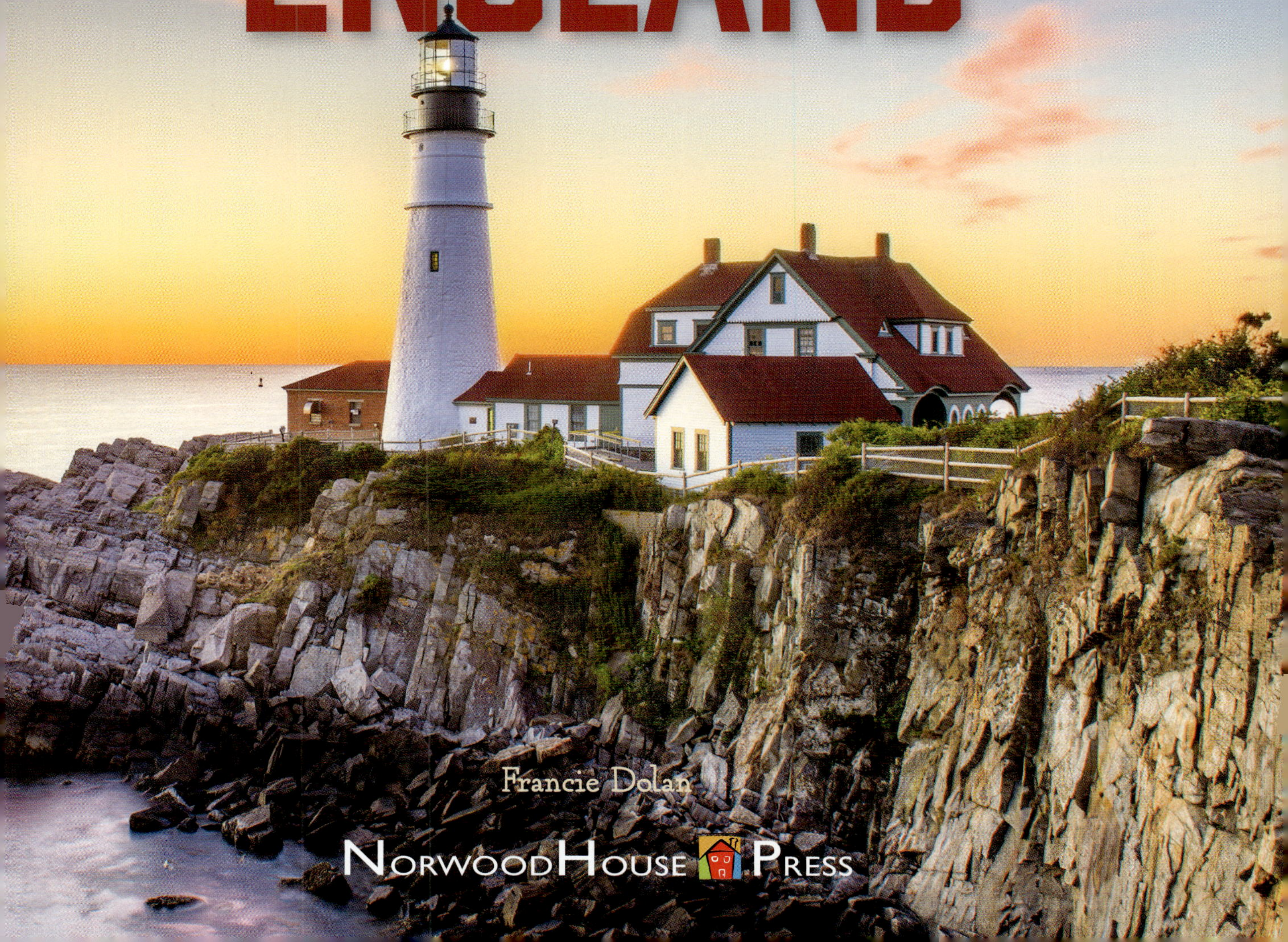

Francie Dolan

NorwoodHouse Press

Cataloging-in-Publication Data

Names: Dolan, Francie.
Title: New England / Francie Dolan.
Description: Buffalo, NY : Norwood House Press, 2027. | Series: Regions of America | Includes glossary and index.
Identifiers: ISBN 9781978581135 (pbk.) | ISBN 9781978581142 (library bound) | ISBN 9781978581159 (ebook)
Subjects: LCSH: New England--Juvenile literature.
Classification: LCC F4.3 D65 2027 | DDC 974--dc23

Published in 2027 by
Norwood House Press
2544 Clinton Street
Buffalo, NY 14224

Designer: Rhea Magaro
Editor: Tricia Hoffman

Photo credits: Cover, p. 1 Sean Pavone/Shutterstock.com; p. 5 Steven Noroian/Shutterstock.com; p. 6 Artography/Shutterstock.com; p. 7 Albert Pego/Shutterstock.com; p. 8 Jayne Lipkovich/Shutterstock.com; p. 10 Jerry Gantar/Shutterstock.com; p. 11 Jerry Gantar/Shutterstock.com; p. 12 Wikipedia; p. 13 Detroit Publishing Company Collection; p. 14 WoodysPhotos/Shutterstock.com; p. 15 Wangkun Jia/Shutterstock.com; p. 17 Felix Lipov/Shutterstock.com; p. 18 NayaDadara/Shutterstock.com; p. 21 Ann Stryzhekin/Shutterstock.com;

Printed in the United States of America

CPSIA compliance information: Batch #CSNHP27: For further information contact Norwood House Press at 1-800-237-9932.

TABLE OF CONTENTS

WHERE IS NEW ENGLAND?

New England is a **region** of the United States. It has six states.

New England

THE LAND

New England is in the northeast corner of the country. Three of its states share a border with Canada.

There are many beaches, but not many good days for swimming. Summers are short. Winters are long and harsh.

All the states, except Vermont, border the Atlantic Ocean. The long **coastline** is jagged and uneven. It has many **inlets** and bays.

There are windy beaches. There are craggy cliffs and **coves**. Lighthouses warn sailors about the rocky shore.

The Appalachian Mountains extend into New England. They include Mount Washington in New Hampshire. It is the tallest peak in the region.

Much of New England is covered by **dense** forests.

THE PEOPLE

Indigenous people once lived across the region. Some tribes were the Pequot and Wampanoag.

The first **settlers** from England landed here after crossing the ocean. It reminded the settlers of home. That's how the region got its name.

Many people live in small towns and villages. Some work on fishing boats or harvest maple syrup.

Many people live in cities. More than four million people live in and around Boston, Massachusetts. It has some of the most well-known **universities** in the country.

THINGS TO SEE AND DO

In Newport, Rhode Island, you can stroll along the Cliff Walk. You'll see old **mansions**, the rocky shore, and crashing waves.

You can take a **ferry** to Martha's Vineyard. The island is off the coast of Massachusetts. It has a long history as a vacation spot for Black American families.

You can visit Acadia National Park in Maine. You can climb to the top of Cadillac Mountain. From here, you can be one of the first people in the U.S. to see the sunrise.

GLOSSARY

coastline (KOHST-line): the place where the land and the ocean meet; the outline of the coast

coves (koves): small, sheltered inlets along the coast

dense (dens): thick; tightly packed together

ferry (FER-ee): a boat that regularly carries people across a stretch of water

Indigenous (in-DI-juh-nuhs): the earliest known people to live in a place

inlets (IN-lets): narrow bodies of water that lead inland from a larger body of water, such as an ocean

mansions (MAN-shuhnz): large, impressive houses that were often built long ago

settlers (SET-luhrz): people who make their homes in a new place and try to build communities there

region (REE-juhn): an area or territory; part of a country

universities (yoo-nuh-VUR-si-teez): schools where people can go after high school to earn degrees, do research, or learn a profession such as law or medicine

THINKING QUESTIONS

1. How did New England get its name?
2. Describe the coastline of New England.
3. Name a big city in New England.
4. Name one Native American tribe from New England.
5. What can you do at Acadia National Park?

INDEX

ABOUT THE AUTHOR

Francie Dolan is a writer from Seattle, Washington. She loves American history and trivia. It is her goal to travel to all 50 states, visit their capital cities, and eat a special food from each place.